EMMANUEL JOSEPH

The Invisible Mapmakers, How Billionaires Quietly Redraw Industries and Redefine the World

Copyright © 2025 by Emmanuel Joseph

All rights reserved. No part of this publication may be reproduced, stored or transmitted in any form or by any means, electronic, mechanical, photocopying, recording, scanning, or otherwise without written permission from the publisher. It is illegal to copy this book, post it to a website, or distribute it by any other means without permission.

First edition

This book was professionally typeset on Reedsy.
Find out more at reedsy.com

Contents

1	Chapter 1: The Secret Cartographers	1
2	Chapter 2: Rise of the Tech Titans	3
3	Chapter 3: Financial Alchemists	5
4	Chapter 4: Media Moguls and the Information Age	7
5	Chapter 5: Industrial Innovators	9
6	Chapter 6: Philanthropy or Influence?	11
7	Chapter 7: Shaping the Future with AI and Automation	13
8	Chapter 8: The Healthcare Revolutionaries	15
9	Chapter 9: Environmental Pioneers	17
10	Chapter 10: Real Estate Tycoons	19
11	Chapter 11: The Power of Connectivity	21
12	Chapter 12: The Disruptors	23
13	Chapter 13: Cultural and Artistic Patrons	25
14	Chapter 14: Political Kingmakers	27
15	Chapter 15: Education Innovators	29
16	Chapter 16: The Global Impact	31
17	Chapter 17: The Future of Influence	33

1

Chapter 1: The Secret Cartographers

In the shadowy realms where power and influence converge, there exists an elite cadre known as the secret cartographers. These are not your conventional mapmakers, plotting geographical coordinates and physical boundaries. Instead, they are the invisible architects of industries, the unseen hands that mold economies and societies. These billionaires wield influence with a precision that redraws borders not with ink, but through strategic innovation, investments, and power plays.

From opulent boardrooms and discreet private jets, they orchestrate the movements that shape our world. Their decisions, often made behind closed doors, resonate far beyond the confines of their exclusive circles. The ripples of their actions spread through economies, reshaping the very fabric of global industries. They are the titans who move markets with a word, who command legions of followers with a mere gesture. Their influence is both profound and elusive, a testament to their ability to operate in the shadows.

Within this clandestine network, the boundaries between industries blur. Technology giants venture into finance, media moguls diversify into healthcare, and industrialists explore the frontiers of renewable energy. The secret cartographers are adept at navigating these intersections, leveraging their diverse portfolios to create synergies that amplify their reach. They possess an uncanny ability to foresee trends and capitalize on opportunities before they become apparent to the world at large.

The global stage is their canvas, and they are the masterful artists who paint with the brushstrokes of innovation and disruption. Their influence extends to the very core of modern society, shaping the narratives that define our collective consciousness. Through strategic investments and acquisitions, they mold the future, guiding the evolution of industries with a deft hand. These billionaires are not just observers; they are the architects of change, the pioneers who push the boundaries of what is possible.

As we delve deeper into the world of the secret cartographers, we uncover the intricate web of connections that bind them. From alliances forged in the crucible of competition to partnerships born of mutual ambition, their networks are as complex as they are powerful. The invisible mapmakers operate with a level of sophistication that transcends conventional business practices, creating a new paradigm of influence and control.

This is just the beginning of our journey into the enigmatic world of the invisible mapmakers. As we progress through the chapters, we will explore the rise of tech titans, the alchemy of financial wizards, the media moguls who shape our perceptions, and much more. The story of these billionaires is one of power, ambition, and the relentless pursuit of innovation. They are the quiet architects of our world, the unseen forces that define our reality.

2

Chapter 2: Rise of the Tech Titans

Silicon Valley, once a sleepy orchard, is now the heart of technological innovation. The transformation from dreamers tinkering in garages to industry giants is a tale of ambition, risk-taking, and unparalleled vision. These tech titans envisioned a digital world, one where the boundaries of communication, commerce, and entertainment would be redefined. Their journey from nascent startups to global dominators showcases their ability to foresee trends and shape the future.

Steve Jobs, Bill Gates, and Mark Zuckerberg are just a few names that have become synonymous with this revolution. Their creations, from the personal computer to social media, have not only disrupted traditional industries but have also created entirely new markets. The rise of smartphones, cloud computing, and artificial intelligence are testaments to their relentless pursuit of innovation. These tech titans are not just inventors; they are visionaries who see possibilities where others see limitations.

The impact of these innovations extends beyond the products themselves. The digital age has transformed how we live, work, and interact. E-commerce has revolutionized retail, social media has reshaped communication, and big data has redefined business strategies. These tech giants have a profound influence on society, creating new paradigms and challenging existing norms. Their ability to adapt and innovate continuously sets them apart in a rapidly evolving landscape.

THE INVISIBLE MAPMAKERS, HOW BILLIONAIRES QUIETLY REDRAW INDUSTRIES AND REDEFINE THE WORLD

As we explore the stories of these tech titans, we uncover the strategies that propelled them to success. From securing venture capital to navigating regulatory challenges, their journeys are marked by resilience and adaptability. They have not only created wealth but have also paved the way for future generations of entrepreneurs. Their legacy is a testament to the power of vision, determination, and the relentless pursuit of progress.

3

Chapter 3: Financial Alchemists

In the world of finance, there are those who possess the Midas touch, turning numbers into gold. These financial alchemists have mastered the art of manipulating markets, creating financial instruments, and reimagining banking. Through hedge funds, private equity, and venture capital, they wield immense power over the global economy. Their influence extends beyond mere wealth, shaping the very foundations of modern finance.

Warren Buffett, George Soros, and Ray Dalio are among the luminaries of this elite group. Their strategies, from value investing to market speculation, have set new benchmarks in the financial world. The ability to predict market trends, identify undervalued assets, and manage risk are hallmarks of their success. They are not merely participants in the market; they are its architects, influencing its direction with their decisions.

The financial alchemists are also known for their innovative approaches to investment. They have pioneered new financial instruments, such as derivatives and structured products, that have transformed the landscape of finance. These tools, while complex, offer new avenues for profit and risk management. The ability to leverage these instruments effectively sets these alchemists apart from the rest.

The impact of their decisions is felt across the global economy. From stock market rallies to economic downturns, their influence is pervasive. They have the power to create wealth on an unprecedented scale, but with great power comes great responsibility. The financial alchemists must navigate the fine line between profit and ethics, ensuring that their actions contribute positively to the world.

4

Chapter 4: Media Moguls and the Information Age

In the age of information, those who control the flow of data hold unparalleled power. Media moguls, with their vast empires of newspapers, television networks, and digital platforms, shape the narratives that define our world. They are the gatekeepers of information, influencing public opinion and cultural perceptions. Their impact extends beyond the headlines, reaching into the very fabric of society.

Rupert Murdoch, Ted Turner, and Jeff Bezos are among the most influential media magnates. Their control over media conglomerates allows them to shape the discourse on politics, culture, and social issues. The ability to influence public opinion through editorial choices and content curation is a potent tool. These media moguls are not just business leaders; they are the architects of the information age.

The rise of digital media has further amplified their influence. The internet has transformed how we consume information, with social media platforms playing a pivotal role. Media moguls have adeptly navigated this transition, expanding their reach through online platforms and streaming services. The ability to adapt to changing technologies and consumer preferences is key to their continued dominance.

However, with great power comes significant responsibility. The control over information carries ethical implications, from issues of bias and misinformation to the impact on democracy. Media moguls must balance their business interests with the duty to provide accurate and fair reporting. The future of the information age depends on their ability to navigate these challenges responsibly.

5

Chapter 5: Industrial Innovators

The industrial landscape has been shaped by visionaries who have redefined manufacturing and production. These industrial innovators have turned assembly lines into global powerhouses, revolutionizing how goods are made and distributed. Their contributions to efficiency, automation, and supply chain management have transformed industries and economies.

Henry Ford, Elon Musk, and Jack Welch are among the most notable figures in this realm. Their innovations, from the introduction of the assembly line to the development of electric vehicles, have set new standards in manufacturing. The ability to optimize production processes and integrate cutting-edge technologies is a hallmark of their success. They are not just manufacturers; they are pioneers who have reimagined the possibilities of industry.

The impact of their innovations extends beyond the factory floor. The rise of automation and robotics has reshaped the labor market, creating new opportunities and challenges. The ability to produce goods at scale and with greater efficiency has driven economic growth and global trade. These industrial innovators have created new paradigms in manufacturing, pushing the boundaries of what is possible.

As we explore their stories, we uncover the strategies and philosophies that underpin their success. From lean manufacturing principles to disruptive innovation, their approaches are marked by a relentless pursuit of improvement. Their legacy is one of transformation, not only in how products are made but in how industries evolve.

These chapters provide a glimpse into the world of the invisible mapmakers. Each chapter delves deeper into the stories of these billionaires, uncovering the strategies and influences that shape our world. As we continue this journey, we will explore the realms of philanthropy, environmental sustainability, political influence, and more. The story of these billionaires is one of power, ambition, and the relentless pursuit of innovation. They are the quiet architects of our world, the unseen forces that define our reality.

6

Chapter 6: Philanthropy or Influence?

The dual-edged sword of billionaire philanthropy often blurs the line between genuine altruism and strategic influence. In the vast halls of power, where wealth mingles with policy and societal advancement, the intentions behind charitable giving can be complex. While some billionaires genuinely strive to make a positive impact, others use philanthropy as a tool to extend their influence and shape public policy.

Take Bill and Melinda Gates, for instance. Their foundation has funneled billions into global health initiatives, education, and poverty alleviation. The impact of their generosity is undeniably profound, touching lives across the globe. Yet, this significant influence also raises questions about accountability and the privatization of public policy. Philanthropy, in this context, becomes more than just charity; it becomes a powerful force that can shape societal priorities and norms.

On the other side of the spectrum, there are billionaires like George Soros, whose philanthropic endeavors through the Open Society Foundations have supported democratic governance, human rights, and education across numerous countries. While his contributions have fostered positive change, they have also sparked controversy and opposition, highlighting the tension between philanthropy and influence.

The motivations behind these philanthropic efforts are multifaceted. Some billionaires are driven by a genuine desire to give back to society, to create a legacy that transcends their wealth. Others see philanthropy as a strategic tool to influence policy, gain public favor, or mitigate negative perceptions. The interplay between these motivations creates a complex landscape where the true impact of philanthropy can be difficult to discern.

The ethical considerations of billionaire philanthropy are equally complex. While the infusion of private wealth into public causes can lead to significant advancements, it can also lead to a concentration of power in the hands of a few. The role of philanthropy in shaping education, healthcare, and social policies necessitates a careful balance between private influence and public accountability. The challenge lies in ensuring that the interests of a few do not overshadow the needs of the many.

7

Chapter 7: Shaping the Future with AI and Automation

At the forefront of technological innovation, a select group of billionaires is driving the evolution of artificial intelligence (AI) and automation. These visionaries are harnessing the power of cutting-edge technologies to revolutionize industries, enhance efficiencies, and redefine the future of work. Their investments and innovations are not only transforming existing sectors but also creating entirely new ones.

Elon Musk, with his ventures in AI and autonomous vehicles, stands as a prominent figure in this landscape. Tesla's advancements in self-driving technology and robotics exemplify the transformative potential of AI and automation. Similarly, companies like Google, led by visionaries like Larry Page and Sergey Brin, are pioneering AI research and applications that span healthcare, finance, and beyond.

The promise of AI and automation lies in their ability to enhance productivity, reduce costs, and unlock new levels of innovation. In manufacturing, automation has already revolutionized production processes, enabling precision and efficiency on an unprecedented scale. In healthcare, AI is driving breakthroughs in diagnostics, personalized medicine, and drug discovery, offering the potential to save lives and improve outcomes.

However, the rapid advancement of these technologies also raises significant challenges. Ethical dilemmas, such as the impact on employment and privacy concerns, necessitate careful consideration. The automation of tasks traditionally performed by humans has led to concerns about job displacement and economic inequality. The ethical use of AI, including issues of bias and accountability, requires a robust framework to ensure that these technologies benefit society as a whole.

As we explore the world of AI and automation, we uncover the strategies and visions of the billionaires who are driving this revolution. Their ability to foresee the potential of these technologies and invest in their development sets them apart as pioneers. The future they envision is one where AI and automation are seamlessly integrated into our daily lives, enhancing our capabilities and creating new opportunities.

8

Chapter 8: The Healthcare Revolutionaries

In the realm of healthcare, a new generation of billionaires is spearheading a revolution that promises to transform how we understand, treat, and prevent diseases. These healthcare revolutionaries are leveraging their wealth and influence to drive medical innovation, improve healthcare accessibility, and address global health challenges.

Bill Gates, through the Bill and Melinda Gates Foundation, has become a prominent figure in global health initiatives. His foundation's investments in vaccine development, infectious disease research, and healthcare infrastructure have had a profound impact on public health. Similarly, biotech entrepreneurs like Patrick Soon-Shiong and Elizabeth Holmes (despite her controversies) have pushed the boundaries of medical science with their pioneering work in cancer treatment and diagnostics.

The contributions of these healthcare billionaires extend beyond financial investments. They bring a visionary approach to solving complex health challenges, often collaborating with governments, research institutions, and other stakeholders. Their efforts have led to significant advancements in drug development, medical technology, and healthcare delivery, improving the lives of millions.

However, the intersection of wealth and healthcare also raises ethical considerations. The influence of billionaires in shaping healthcare policies and priorities can lead to concerns about equity and access. The privatization of medical research and the commercialization of healthcare solutions can create disparities in access to life-saving treatments. Ensuring that the benefits of healthcare innovations are equitably distributed remains a critical challenge.

As we delve into the stories of these healthcare revolutionaries, we uncover the motivations, challenges, and triumphs that define their journeys. Their impact on global health is a testament to the potential of visionary leadership and the power of innovation to create a healthier future for all.

9

Chapter 9: Environmental Pioneers

In the face of climate change and environmental degradation, a group of billionaires is championing sustainability and green technologies. These environmental pioneers are leveraging their influence and resources to drive initiatives that promote conservation, renewable energy, and sustainable practices. Their efforts are not only addressing pressing environmental challenges but also creating profitable industries that contribute to a greener future.

Elon Musk, with his ventures in electric vehicles and solar energy, stands as a leading figure in this movement. Tesla's electric cars and SolarCity's renewable energy solutions exemplify the potential for sustainable technologies to reshape industries. Similarly, billionaires like Jeff Bezos and Richard Branson are investing in space exploration and clean energy, pushing the boundaries of what is possible.

The investments in renewable energy, such as wind, solar, and hydropower, are transforming the energy landscape. These green technologies offer the promise of reducing carbon emissions, combating climate change, and creating sustainable sources of energy. The shift towards sustainability is not only an environmental imperative but also an economic opportunity, driving job creation and fostering innovation.

However, the path to a sustainable future is not without challenges. The transition from fossil fuels to renewable energy requires significant investments, policy support, and technological advancements. The role of billionaires in shaping environmental policies and driving sustainable practices necessitates a careful balance between economic interests and environmental stewardship. The ethical considerations of their influence and the need for accountability are critical in ensuring that sustainability efforts benefit society as a whole.

As we explore the stories of these environmental pioneers, we uncover their visions, strategies, and impact. Their contributions to sustainability and green technologies are a testament to the potential of visionary leadership and the power of innovation to create a more sustainable future.

The journey through the world of the invisible mapmakers continues. Each chapter delves deeper into the stories of these billionaires, uncovering the strategies and influences that shape our world. As we proceed, we will explore the realms of real estate, connectivity, cultural patronage, political influence, and more. The story of these billionaires is one of power, ambition, and the relentless pursuit of innovation. They are the quiet architects of our world, the unseen forces that define our reality.

continue

10

Chapter 10: Real Estate Tycoons

Real estate is more than just bricks and mortar; it's about vision, ambition, and the power to shape urban landscapes. The billionaires who dominate this realm have transformed cities and redefined the concept of real estate. Their influence extends beyond property development, impacting housing markets, urban planning, and community dynamics.

Donald Trump, Sam Zell, and Harry Macklowe are iconic names in the real estate industry. Their ventures range from luxury skyscrapers to expansive commercial properties, reshaping skylines and creating urban landmarks. These tycoons possess an uncanny ability to identify undervalued properties, envision their potential, and execute ambitious development projects that redefine cityscapes.

The strategies employed by these real estate moguls are multifaceted. They navigate complex regulatory environments, secure financing from diverse sources, and leverage their networks to bring projects to fruition. Their success hinges on their ability to anticipate market trends, adapt to changing economic conditions, and create properties that meet the evolving needs of urban dwellers and businesses.

However, the impact of their developments is not without controversy. Gentrification, displacement, and affordability are significant issues associated with large-scale real estate projects. The influx of high-end developments can lead to rising property values, often pushing out longtime residents and altering the character of neighborhoods. Balancing the pursuit of profit with social responsibility is a delicate challenge for real estate tycoons.

As we delve into the stories of these real estate magnates, we uncover the visions, challenges, and triumphs that define their journeys. Their influence on urban landscapes is a testament to the power of visionary leadership and the potential of real estate to shape the future of cities.

11

Chapter 11: The Power of Connectivity

In an increasingly interconnected world, the billionaires driving the communications revolution wield immense power. From telecommunications to satellite networks, these visionaries are connecting the globe, transforming how we communicate, access information, and interact with one another.

Carlos Slim, Mukesh Ambani, and Elon Musk are at the forefront of this revolution. Their ventures, such as America Movil, Reliance Jio, and SpaceX's Starlink, are bridging the digital divide and expanding internet access to underserved regions. The ability to provide reliable and affordable connectivity is not just a technological achievement; it's a catalyst for economic growth, education, and social development.

The impact of global connectivity extends beyond individual users. It enables the digital economy, supports remote work and education, and fosters innovation across industries. The rise of 5G technology, the proliferation of Internet of Things (IoT) devices, and the expansion of satellite internet are reshaping the communications landscape, creating new opportunities and challenges.

However, the power of connectivity also raises significant ethical considerations. Issues of privacy, data security, and digital inclusion are paramount in a connected world. The influence of billionaires in shaping the regulatory environment and setting standards for connectivity must be balanced with the need to protect users' rights and ensure equitable access.

As we explore the stories of these connectivity pioneers, we uncover their visions, strategies, and impact. Their contributions to global communication are a testament to the potential of visionary leadership and the power of technology to create a more connected world.

12

Chapter 12: The Disruptors

Billionaires who challenge the status quo and create new paradigms are often seen as disruptors. These mavericks defy conventional wisdom, innovate relentlessly, and redefine entire industries. Their audacious ventures, from space exploration to transportation, are pushing the boundaries of what is possible and creating new frontiers of opportunity.

Elon Musk, with his ventures in electric vehicles, space travel, and renewable energy, epitomizes the spirit of disruption. Tesla's electric cars have transformed the automotive industry, while SpaceX's reusable rockets are revolutionizing space travel. Similarly, Jeff Bezos' Amazon has redefined retail, logistics, and cloud computing, setting new standards for innovation and customer experience.

The journey of disruptors is marked by bold risks and relentless pursuit of their vision. They often face skepticism, regulatory challenges, and fierce competition. However, their ability to innovate, adapt, and persevere sets them apart. The impact of their ventures extends beyond their respective industries, driving economic growth, technological advancement, and societal change.

The ethical considerations of disruption are complex. The rapid pace of innovation can lead to unintended consequences, such as job displacement and market monopolization. Balancing the drive for progress with the need for responsible innovation is a critical challenge for disruptors. Ensuring that the benefits of innovation are broadly shared and that potential harms are mitigated requires a thoughtful and proactive approach.

As we explore the stories of these disruptors, we uncover their visions, strategies, and impact. Their contributions to innovation are a testament to the potential of visionary leadership and the power of disruption to create new possibilities.

13

Chapter 13: Cultural and Artistic Patrons

The influence of billionaires extends beyond business and technology; it reaches into the realms of arts, culture, and entertainment. Cultural and artistic patrons use their wealth to support creativity, shape cultural narratives, and preserve artistic heritage. Their patronage not only fosters innovation in the arts but also influences public perception and societal values.

David Geffen, Paul Allen, and Peggy Guggenheim are notable figures in the world of cultural patronage. Their contributions to museums, galleries, theaters, and film have left an indelible mark on the cultural landscape. The ability to support artistic endeavors, from funding new productions to preserving historic works, is a powerful tool for shaping cultural narratives and promoting creativity.

The role of cultural and artistic patrons is multifaceted. They provide financial support, mentorship, and platforms for emerging artists. Their investments in cultural institutions and creative projects foster innovation, enhance public access to the arts, and preserve cultural heritage. The impact of their patronage extends beyond individual artists, influencing public perception, cultural trends, and societal values.

However, the influence of cultural patrons also raises ethical considerations. The power to shape cultural narratives and public perception carries significant responsibility. Ensuring that patronage promotes diversity, inclusivity, and artistic integrity is critical. The potential for conflicts of interest, bias, and commercialization must be carefully managed to preserve the integrity of artistic endeavors.

As we explore the stories of these cultural and artistic patrons, we uncover their visions, strategies, and impact. Their contributions to the arts are a testament to the potential of visionary leadership and the power of creativity to enrich society.

The journey through the world of the invisible mapmakers continues. Each chapter delves deeper into the stories of these billionaires, uncovering the strategies and influences that shape our world. As we proceed, we will explore the realms of political influence, education innovation, global impact, and the future of influence. The story of these billionaires is one of power, ambition, and the relentless pursuit of innovation. They are the quiet architects of our world, the unseen forces that define our reality.

14

Chapter 14: Political Kingmakers

In the complex interplay between wealth and politics, a select group of billionaires wields significant influence as political kingmakers. Their ability to shape political landscapes through campaign financing, lobbying, and policy-making positions them as powerful players in the world of governance. These billionaires leverage their resources to support candidates, influence legislation, and drive political agendas that align with their interests.

The Koch brothers, Charles and David, are prominent examples of political kingmakers. Their extensive network of advocacy groups, think tanks, and political action committees has had a profound impact on American politics. Similarly, Michael Bloomberg's foray into political influence, both as a mayor and a philanthropist, highlights the potential for billionaires to shape public policy and drive political change.

The strategies employed by these political kingmakers are multifaceted. They invest in political campaigns, fund grassroots movements, and engage in extensive lobbying efforts. Their ability to mobilize resources and influence public opinion allows them to shape the direction of political discourse and policy decisions. The impact of their involvement is far-reaching, affecting everything from regulatory frameworks to social policies.

However, the influence of political kingmakers raises significant ethical considerations. The concentration of political power in the hands of a few wealthy individuals can undermine democratic principles and create disparities in representation. The potential for conflicts of interest, undue influence, and erosion of public trust necessitates a careful balance between political engagement and ethical responsibility. Ensuring transparency, accountability, and equitable representation is critical in preserving the integrity of democratic processes.

As we delve into the stories of these political kingmakers, we uncover their motivations, strategies, and impact. Their influence on political landscapes is a testament to the power of wealth in shaping governance and the importance of ethical considerations in political engagement.

15

Chapter 15: Education Innovators

Education is the cornerstone of societal progress, and a group of visionary billionaires is driving innovation in this critical field. These education innovators leverage their resources and influence to transform how we learn, teach, and access knowledge. Their investments in educational technology, online learning platforms, and educational reforms are creating new opportunities for students and educators alike.

Bill Gates, through the Bill and Melinda Gates Foundation, has been a major proponent of educational reform. His foundation's initiatives in improving K-12 education, supporting teacher development, and promoting college readiness have had a significant impact on the education system. Similarly, Laurene Powell Jobs' Emerson Collective invests in innovative educational approaches, including personalized learning and school redesign.

The contributions of these education innovators extend beyond financial investments. They bring a visionary approach to addressing the challenges and opportunities in education. By leveraging technology, data analytics, and innovative pedagogies, they aim to create more equitable and effective learning environments. Their efforts are driving advancements in digital learning, personalized instruction, and educational accessibility.

However, the intersection of wealth and education also raises ethical considerations. The influence of billionaires in shaping educational policies and priorities can create disparities in access and representation. Ensuring that educational innovations are inclusive, equitable, and aligned with the needs of diverse student populations is critical. The role of public accountability and stakeholder engagement is essential in guiding the direction of educational reforms.

As we explore the stories of these education innovators, we uncover their visions, strategies, and impact. Their contributions to education are a testament to the potential of visionary leadership and the power of innovation to create a brighter future for learners.

16

Chapter 16: The Global Impact

The actions of billionaires reverberate across the globe, influencing economies, cultures, and societies. Their ability to drive global change through investments, philanthropy, and innovation positions them as key players on the world stage. The interconnectedness of their endeavors creates ripple effects that shape the trajectory of global development.

The global impact of billionaires is evident in various sectors. From Elon Musk's ventures in renewable energy and space exploration to Bill Gates' efforts in global health and poverty alleviation, their contributions are transformative. Their ability to mobilize resources, drive innovation, and address global challenges positions them as influential figures in shaping the future.

However, the global influence of billionaires also raises significant ethical considerations. The concentration of wealth and power in the hands of a few individuals can create disparities in representation and access. The potential for unintended consequences, such as market disruptions and social inequalities, necessitates a careful balance between ambition and responsibility. Ensuring that the benefits of global initiatives are equitably distributed and aligned with the needs of diverse populations is critical.

As we explore the stories of these global influencers, we uncover their motivations, strategies, and impact. Their contributions to global development are a testament to the potential of visionary leadership and the power of innovation to create a more equitable and sustainable world.

17

Chapter 17: The Future of Influence

As we look to the future, the role of billionaires in shaping industries and the world continues to evolve. The potential for new technologies, industries, and global challenges creates opportunities for a new generation of influential figures to emerge. The future of influence is marked by the interplay between innovation, ethics, and the pursuit of societal progress.

The future role of billionaires in shaping industries will be driven by their ability to anticipate and capitalize on emerging trends. From advancements in artificial intelligence and biotechnology to the exploration of space and sustainable development, the potential for transformative innovation is vast. The ability to leverage resources, drive research, and foster collaboration will be key in navigating the complexities of the future.

However, the future of influence also raises significant ethical considerations. The concentration of power and wealth necessitates a careful balance between ambition and responsibility. The potential for unintended consequences, ethical dilemmas, and social disparities requires a proactive and thoughtful approach. Ensuring that the benefits of innovation are broadly shared and aligned with societal needs is critical in preserving the integrity of future endeavors.

As we contemplate the future of influence, we recognize the importance of visionary leadership, ethical responsibility, and the relentless pursuit of progress. The stories of the billionaires we have explored are a testament to the power of innovation and the potential for positive change. They are the quiet architects of our world, the unseen forces that define our reality.

Book Description: The Invisible Mapmakers: How Billionaires Quietly Redraw Industries and Redefine the World

In "The Invisible Mapmakers: How Billionaires Quietly Redraw Industries and Redefine the World," delve into the clandestine world of the most powerful billionaires who shape our reality. Far from the public eye, these elites exercise their influence to transform industries and, ultimately, redefine the global landscape. Through innovation, strategic investments, and behind-the-scenes power plays, they move markets and societies, creating ripple effects that touch every corner of our lives.

This book offers an insightful exploration of the secretive lives and groundbreaking contributions of tech titans, financial alchemists, media moguls, and more. Discover how these visionaries, like Steve Jobs, Bill Gates, Warren Buffett, and Rupert Murdoch, rose to prominence and used their unparalleled foresight to disrupt traditional industries and create new ones. From the digital age's revolutionary inventions to the intricacies of modern finance, their stories reveal the masterful strokes of the invisible mapmakers.

Each chapter delves into a different realm influenced by these billionaires, including healthcare, environmental sustainability, real estate, and global connectivity. Readers will gain an understanding of the ethical dilemmas, societal impacts, and future potentials driven by their actions. Learn about the philanthropic endeavors that blur the lines between altruism and strategic influence, and the cultural patronage that shapes our artistic landscapes.

"The Invisible Mapmakers" uncovers the intricate web of connections that bind these power players and highlights their role as the unseen architects of change. With a blend of engaging narratives, insightful analysis, and thought-provoking perspectives, this book paints a comprehensive picture of how a select few quietly redraw the boundaries of our world.

www.ingramcontent.com/pod-product-compliance
Lightning Source LLC
LaVergne TN
LVHW020459080526
838202LV00057B/6041